So, What is This Thing?

Well, it's a workbook—but before I tell you what that means,
let me tell you why I made it.

The greatest gift I gave myself in my twenties was a journal. Not only was it my faithful, nonjudgmental companion during solo dinners and travels abroad, but it also carried all the thoughts and feelings I experienced during big moves, career experimentation, dating adventures, and other transformative moments in my life. It was like having a best friend who knew all about me and occasionally offered advice based on what she knew about my past (which was everything). I sat with my journal in coffee shops, on bar stools, on airplanes, in empty apartments. Some pages are crinkly from being soaked with tears, others from splashes of celebratory champagne. I turned to my journal in times of stress, confusion, elation, and boredom to get to know myself better.

Recording my observations—of my surroundings and the inner workings of my mind—is the best way for me to learn more about who I am and what I want. I use it to reflect on past events and to push myself forward.

Today my preferred form of journaling is drawing. I started illustrating in my late twenties as a self-care coping mechanism and a way to bring some joy into every day of my life. Like traditional journaling, it's a powerful way to get to know and express myself, and I also find it very relaxing. People often ask where I get my inspiration for illustrations or how I developed my voice. Putting my experiences down on paper every day, either through writing or drawing, has been the quickest and most delightful way to strengthen my creative muscle It feels so good to sit with myself for a while and get to know a little more about how my heart and mind work.

FRiENDSHiP

PeRSoNaL STYLe

CoMMuTe WoeS

ReJecTioN

Re

I used the observations I'd collected during my twenties to write my first book, *Am I There Yet?*, which is a collection of written and illustrated stories about the heartbreak, joy, confusion, and self-discovery I experienced in early adulthood. Creating the book gave me ownership over my story. For me, *Am I There Yet?* is not only a time capsule of my most formative experiences, but also a peek into how I saw the world during that period of my life; I'm so grateful to have that. I made this workbook to give you the same thing—a special, personal time capsule of your own journey.

Where are you now and where do you want to go next? As the title implies, *Getting There* is meant to capture your internal map. At the beginning of my illustration career (at age twenty-eight!), I remember thinking, I don't really have a style or much to say. Why would anyone be interested in my drawings when so many people do it so much better? I quickly realized there is no difference between someone who likes to draw and someone who considers him- or herself an artist. Anybody with a pen is allowed to create art, and if you're thinking I don't have anything important to say, you're wrong! Nobody can express your feelings better than you do. You're the expert of your inner world, so you get to share that however you want—through stick figures, elaborate oil paintings, photographs, words, poetry, emoji, or anything else—and that is an art. Art is whatever you make it.

The prompts in this workbook are pulled from my work on Instagram and from *Am I There Yet?* I've used all the questions in this workbook at some point to help me navigate my daily life and set my hopes for the future. You'll find templates that I've created to help me explore myself and my surroundings, but the content that completes them is all for you to add. There are small samples on some pages to help you get going.

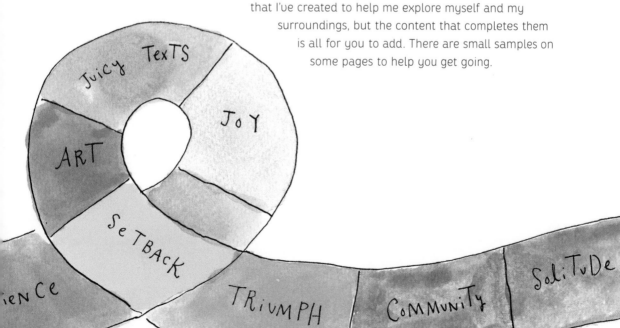

THe DETaiLS

WHeRe aND WHeN?

This workbook is your opportunity to look at your own feelings, thoughts, fears, and desires and make art out of them. I designed it to help you get to know yourself as you are now. Perhaps you can take it as a hot date to your favorite restaurant and pretend it's a dashing lover who is asking you all the right questions (such as, "What is your greatest fear?" Swoon!). I love to dine alone, but I always bring something to do so I'm not allowing my phone to distract me from my ragù. This book is the perfect dinner-date companion, and you might even meet an intriguing person while drawing a portrait of your future self.

You may lean on this workbook during a difficult season of your life. Perhaps you're in a challenging transition between jobs or you're experiencing some heartache. I've been there (950 times, to be exact). I find that journaling during a really intense period of life can help me climb out of a difficult situation and into the bright light of the world again. Once you're able to articulate your experience, you gain control over whatever is happening to you. Likewise, you can use this book to capture a happy time of your life! It's always fun to look back on those sweet months or years when you are in a good place. Hard moments in life are temporary, and so too are the happy ones. It's nice to have time capsules for both. I've found that looking back on my happiest times can be wonderful fuel for getting me through tough challenges later.

How oFTeN?

That's up to you! You could work on it every day for 100 days in a row to develop your voice or a specific artistic skill. If you've always loved writing or drawing but haven't indulged yourself since you were a kid, here's your perfect opportunity. Or you can dip around to different sections and just keep it in your bag and wait for inspiration to strike! It doesn't have to be perfect or precious. In fact, I highly encourage you to spill on it, dog-ear your favorite pages, tear out a prompt and send it to a friend, or give it a battle scar as you stuff it into the seat-back pocket of an airplane. (Why are those always so small?)

WHat Do I NeeD?

I like to use felt-tip pens and watercolors because they're easy and cheap (real talk!), but I'm sure you can think of many other creative ways to respond to these prompts. Making a collage sounds fun, or using photos and stickers works, too. I love simple pencil drawings as much as I love elaborate paintings. You can even switch it up from page to page depending on your mood and what art supplies you might have lying around.

Do I SHaRe iT?

You do not have to offer the world what you record in this workbook, but my greatest hope is that, through getting to know yourself and your desires better, you'll be able to offer the world more of yourself. You and I are both "getting there," but one thing I've found makes the journey a lot easier is taking ownership of your experiences and getting to know yourself very well. Just like your experiences, this journal is 100 percent yours and nobody can tell you how to use it or what to do with it. But can I make a suggestion that you post a photo of your favorite page? (Use the hashtag #gettingthereworkbook.) I'd absolutely love to see it!

Now GeT GoinG!

ANaToMy oF :ME:

RiGHT NOW

Who you are as you begin this workbook?

Fave
Accessory

Comfy
Sweater

Traveling
Shoes

WHat I've Been LeaRNING: _____

_____

_____

WHaT I've Been LiSTeNing To / ReADinG /
WATCHinG: _____

_____

_____

_____

My WeeKDay AcceSSoRieS: _____

_____

_____

My WeeKenD AcceSSoRieS: _____

_____

_____

WHat Else? _____

_____

_____

PEOPLE WHO LIGHT
UP MY LIFE

WHO ILLUMINATES
MY PATH:

_____

WHO HAS BEEN A
FLASHLIGHT IN a DARK TIME:

_____

WHO HAS GREAT
iDEAS:

_____

WHO GIVES ME LIFE:

_____

A WRITER OR ARTIST WHO COMFORTS ME:

_____

SOMEONE WHO BROUGHT ROMANCE INTO MY LIFE:

_____

SOMEONE WHOSE LOVE WASHES OVER ME LIKE LIGHT:

_____

MY GUIDING LIGHT:

_____

To-Do List

☐ Wear the outfit I feel
most comfortable in:

_____

☐ Talk to the friend who lets
me exhale: _____

_____

☐ Enjoy something I used to
do as a kid: _____

_____

☐ Listen to a song I love
to belt: _____

_____

FRiENDSHiP

Fill in this pie chart representing what friendship means to you.
(Social media adoration? Shared hatred of pickles?)

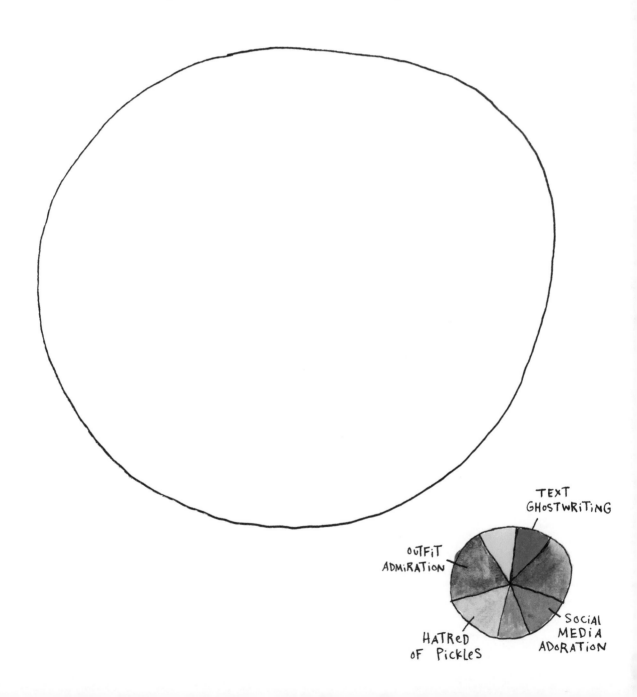

TEXT GHOSTWRITING

OUTFIT ADMIRATION

SOCIAL MEDIA ADORATION

HATRED OF PICKLES

MY :SEASON: HEART

What sights, sounds, memories, and feelings
is this season bringing up for you?

LiFe iN 3 AcTS

Create a visual metaphor of resilience.

1. LiFe iN oNe Piece

2. FaLLS APaRT

3. WHat I DiD wiTH The Pieces

I LiKe To ViSualiZe My LiFe
AS a CoLLecTioN oF SeaSoNS RaTHeR
THaN AS a TiMeLiNe MoViNg FoRWaRD.
IN EveRy SeaSoN, THeRe aRe GoRGeouS
MoMeNTS aND THeRe ARe CHaLLeNGES.
A MoMeNT iN TiMe— JoyFul oR PAiNFuL —
WoN'T LaST FoReveR. USe THiS
KNowleDGe To HeLP you APPReciaTe
THe BeauTy iN YouR LiFe aND Give you
PeRSPecTive oN LiFe's DiFFicuLT TiMeS.

FRee Space

Free Space

FRee Space

FRee Space

MAKING MY CITY
My OWN

Draw a map of where you live, plotting your
favorite and most meaningful spots.

MAP OF _____

KEY:

 = FRiENDS' HoUSES = QUiET SPoTS

 = MeMoRieS 🙂 = HAPPy PLACES

MAP oF _____

FiRST KiSS

PARK

CAFé

CHILDHooD APARTMENT

SCHooL

FACiNG FeaR

Look a fear in the face. What do you want to say to it?

My GReaTeST FeaR iS:

_____

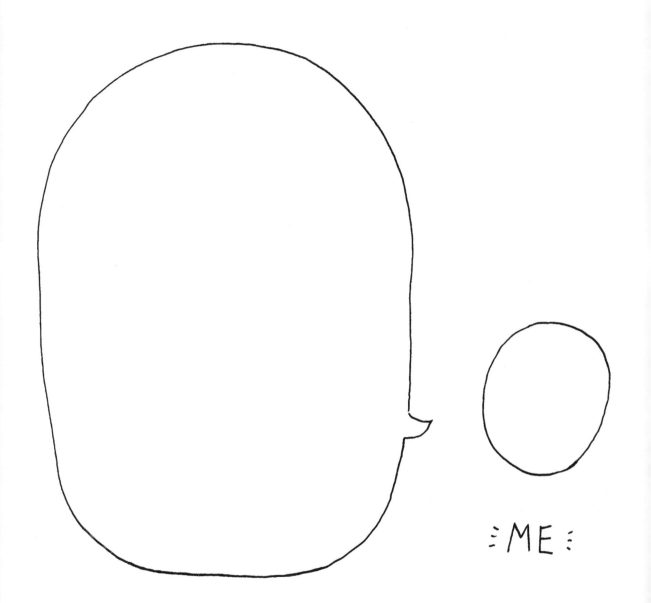

JOBS I'VE HAD

Random jobs teach valuable lessons (like how to make
an almond milk latte). What have your jobs taught you?

FAVORITE COWORKER:

SKILL I LEARNED:

Me AS A

_____

YEAR:

UNIFORM:

New TALENT ACQUIRED:

Me AS A

_____

YEAR:

WORK   SCHEDULE:

SOMETHING   I   LEARNED ABOUT MYSELF:

Me   AS   A

YEAR:

PERK OF THe JOB:

WISDOM   I   GAINED:

ME   AS   A

YEAR:

COMMUTE   HIGHLIGHT:

LESSON   LEARNED:

Me   AS   A

YEAR:

ANaToMy oF The (iMAGiNARY oR REAL) LoVE oF My LiFE

This is your chance to be as ridiculous or thoughtful as you like.
How does this person make you feel? How tall is he? What does she smell like?

GooD COAT

BooKS

THEIR SCENT:

_____

_____

_____

_____

THEIR MOST ATTRACTIVE ACCESSORIES:

_____

_____

_____

_____

OUR DREAM DATE:

_____

_____

_____

To - Do List

:To Be A Good Friend:

☐ Text _____
"I'm Thinking About You"

☐ Invite _____ To Go Dancing!

☐ Attend _____'s Special Event

You're invited ♡

Improv Tonight!

☐ Send Card To _____

☐ Bring Coffee To _____

MY GRoWTH GARDen

What, where, or how are you growing in your life right now?
What is helping it happen? Remember both the sunshine and the rain!

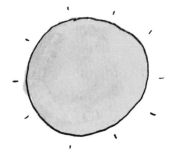

MY FRiENDS

What do three of your friends have in common?
How are they different?

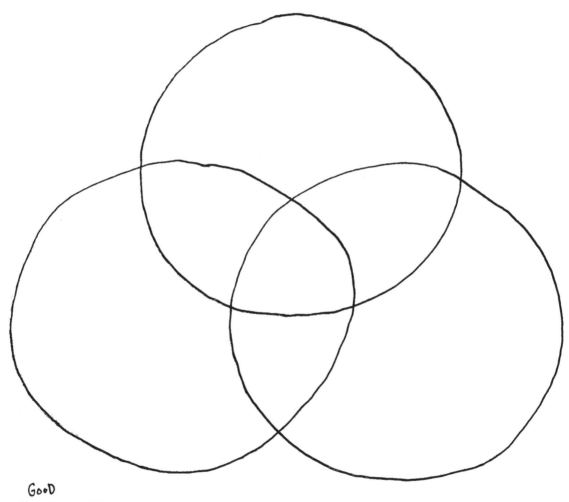

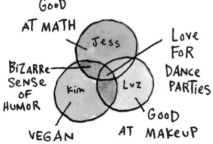

GOOD
AT MATH

BiZARRe
SeNSe
OF
HUMOR

Jess

Kim

Luz

Love
FoR
DANce
PARTies

GOOD
AT MAKeuP

VEGAN

My :PeoPle: HeaRT

Who is in your heart these days?

My LiFe iN BeveRaGeS

MeMoRy 1: CHiLDHooD

DRiNK:

YEAR:

MeMoRy 2: TeeNS

DRiNK:

YEAR:

MeMoRy 3: FRienDSHiP

DRinK:

YEAR:

MeMoRY 4: RoMance

DRinK:

YEAR:

MeMoRy 5: SoLiTuDE

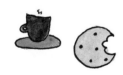

DRinK:

YEAR:

HEALING
FROM ⋮

Plot general progress and, if you like, note specific
people, books, quotes, etc., that have helped along the way.

PROGRESS

TIME

· Solo trip
· Podcast
· Therapy
· Yoga

My TexT ConveRSATioN
wiTH :

Document or imagine a text exchange with a BFF/ex/crush.

MaSTeRiNG

A New SkiLL ꞉

꞉

What made it so intimidating/confusing?

BEFoRe:

Pronouns

Verbs

Accent

slang

Draw your impression of the same skill. What steps helped untangle it?

AFTeR:

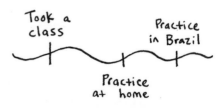

Took a
class
Practice
in Brazil
Practice
at home

MY POWeR TooLS

What are your sources of power—as unlikely as they may be?

My CReaTive PoweR:

_____

_____

My EMoTioNaL PoweR:

_____

_____

My PoweR at WoRK:

_____

_____

My PoweR iN ReLaTioNSHiPS:

_____

_____

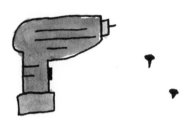

My PoweR in HARD TimeS:

_____

_____

My PoweR in CoNveRSATioN:

_____

_____

MY UNiQve PoweR:

_____

_____

My PoweR To HeLP:

_____

_____

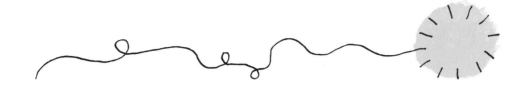

My SuPeR PoweRS ARe SenSiTiviTy, LiFe ExPeRiences EMPATHY, and THe ReLenTLeSS PuRSuiT oF JoY, BuT THEY DiDNT ALwayS FeeL So PoweRFul. Being CALLeD "oveRLy SenSiTive" MoST oF MY LiFe Made Me DouBT MySeLF. My LiFe exPeRience CoMeS FRoM TimeS oF GReat unceRTAinTy. My EMPATHY SPRouTS DiRecTLy FRoM MoMenTS oF DeeP PAin. EMBRace THe PoweR you FinD in unLikeLy PlaceS — You MiGHT JuST FinD a New SuPeRPoweR.

CONFRONTING MY CRITICS

Gain control over biting criticism by responding to that one boss, teacher, stranger, or whomever else here.

My GREATEST CRITIC:

_____

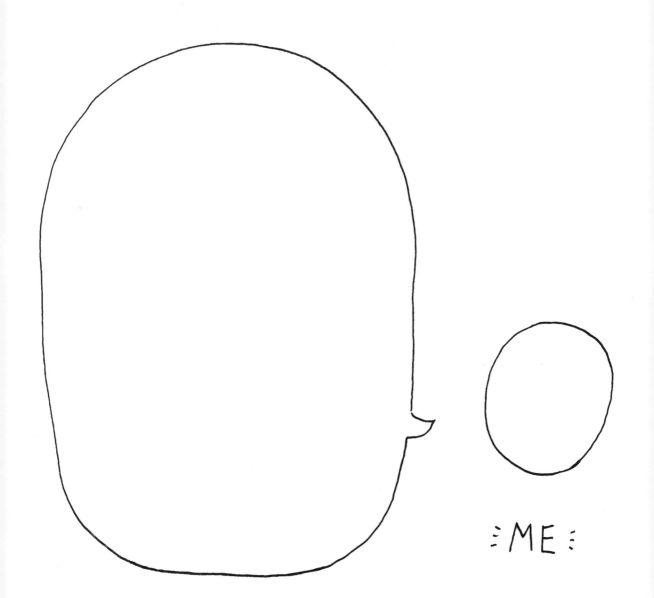

HAPPINESS

HAPPINESS

TIME

KEY:

- ■ FRieNDSHiP
- ▨ ReLaTion SHiP
- ■ CAReeR

- ▨ WHeRe I Live
- ☐ _____
- ☐ _____

A RelATioNSHiP in 3 AcTS

Create a visual metaphor of a relationship you've had.

1.

2.

3.

MY CLOSET MaKeoveR

Draw your current versus ideal closet. Perhaps the ideal reflects the lifestyle you want or the level of organization you admire.

CURRENT:

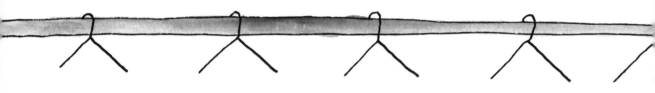

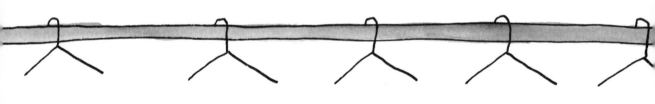

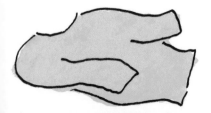

I D E A L :

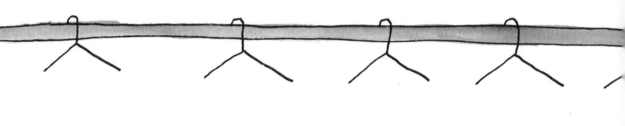

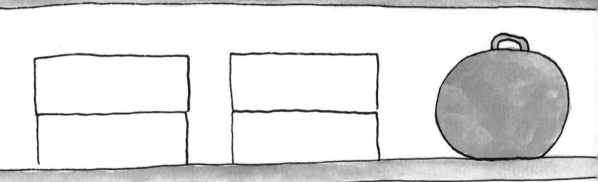

SECReTS

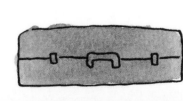

My COMMUNICATIONS TeAM

Who are your conversation cowriters?

EdiToR: _____

CHeeRLeADeR: _____

INTeRPReTeR: _____

EMoJi ConSuLTanT: _____

EMotional SupPoRT: _____

PRiDe iN MYSeLF

What are the little things (like remembering to bring your lunch) and the big things
(the way you handled a tough challenge) that make you proud?

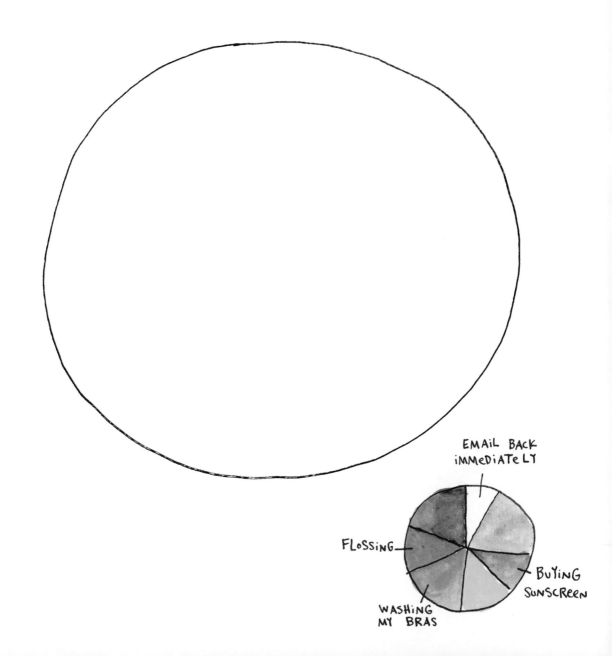

EMAiL BACK
iMMeDiATe LY

FLOSSiNG

BUYiNG
SUNSCReeN

WASHiNG
MY BRAS

My Life in Songs

Which albums or songs have been the soundtrack for your life?

SONG 1:

MEMORY:

_____
YEAR

SONG 2:

MEMORY:

_____
YEAR

SONG 3:

MEMORY:

_____
YEAR

SONG 4:

MEMORY:

_____
YEAR

SONG 5:

MEMORY:

_____
YEAR

SONG 6:

MEMORY:

_____
YEAR

To-Do List

WITH PALS, yourself, OR a SIGNIFICANT OTHER

☐ ReStauRanT To TRy: _____

_____

_____

☐ WALK To TAKe: _____

_____

_____

☐ ThiNG To See: _____

_____

☐ SeaSonal Date To ENJoy: _____

_____

My InSPiRaTioN

What and who inspires you? Create a pie chart of your greatest inspirations for art, love, friendship, home, and life goals.

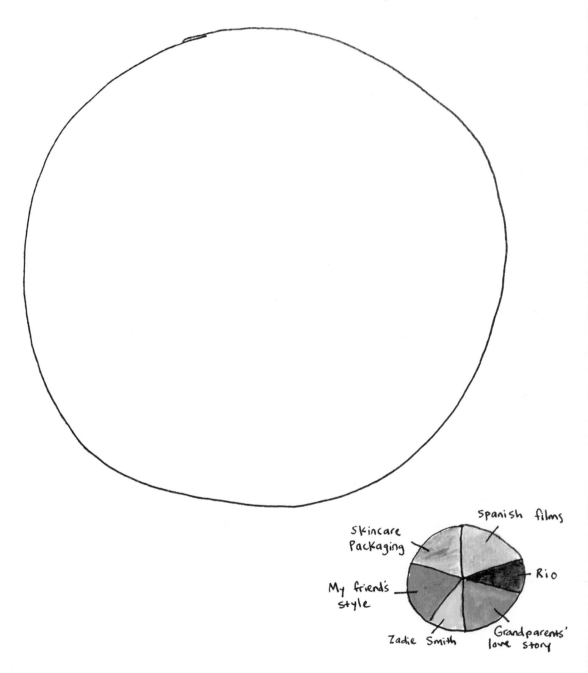

Skincare Packaging

Spanish films

Rio

My friend's style

Zadie Smith

Grandparents' love story

LiFe in 4 SEASonS

Life's seasons mimic the Earth's. What have the seasons of your life taught you?

SPRinG: PlanTing SEEDS

_____

_____

_____

_____

_____

SuMMeR: ABunDance and GRATiTuDe

_____

_____

_____

_____

_____

AUTUMN: LOSS AND SHEDDING

_____

_____

_____

_____

_____

_____

WINTER: QUIET GROWTH

_____

_____

_____

_____

_____

The JouRNey I Took

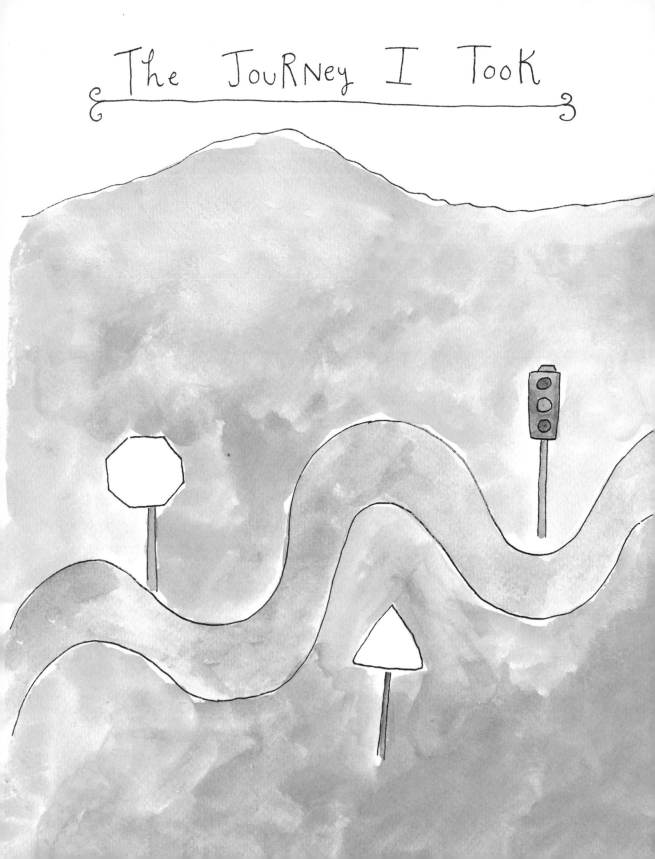

What's something that used to look like a twisting, curvy road—a program you use at work, sheet music, a foreign language—that now looks clear and coherent? Label your road blocks below, and the signs that guided you on your way to the next page.

WELCOME TO

AS I'VE GROWN INTO ADULTHOOD,
MY IDENTITY HAS LESS TO DO WITH
MY ACCOMPLISHMENTS, AND MORE TO DO
WITH WHO I AM AS A PERSON — HOW I
HANDLE TOUGH TIMES, HOW I EMBRACE
JOY, AND HOW I LOVE MY FRIENDS AND
FAMILY. THE QUEST FOR IDENTITY IS
ONGOING, BUT ONE OF MY FAVORITE
PARTS OF MOVING THROUGH THE YEARS
IS LETTING GO OF THE PRESSURE TO
ACCOMPLISH, AND EMBRACING MY DESIRE
TO EXPERIENCE.

FRee Space

FRee Space

Free Space

FRee Space

MY INNER VOICE

Shut down an inner demon holding you back.

My GREATEST DEMON:

_____

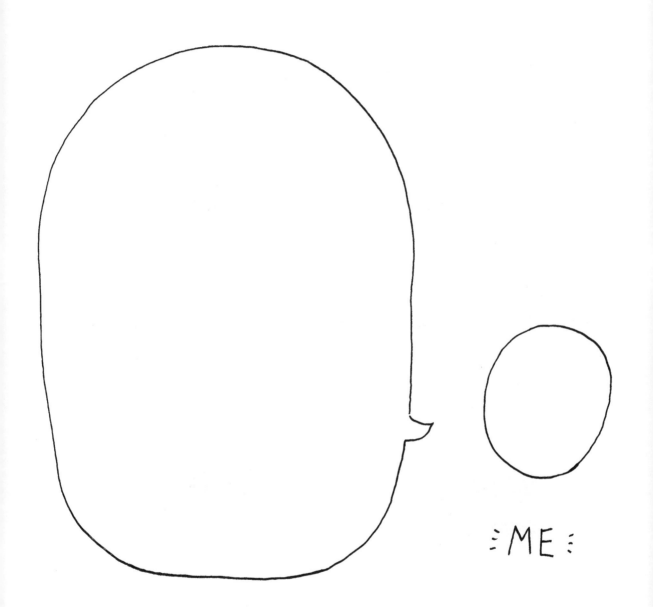

MY GIFTS

What are your special skills, talents, and offerings?

RECiPieNT: _____
GiFT: _____
_____

RECiPieNT: _____
GiFT: _____
_____

RECiPieNT: _____
GiFT: _____
_____

RECiPieNT: _____
GiFT: _____
_____

RECiPiENT: _____
GiFT: _____
_____

RECiPiENT: _____
GiFT: _____
_____

RECiPiENT: _____
GiFT: _____
_____

RECiPiENT: _____
GiFT: _____
_____

My ⬚⬚-Year-oLD HeART

What are all the complicated, sweet, and absurd
things about your exact age right now?

MY WORK CONVERSATION WITH :

Chatting with coworkers—even via instant messaging or sticky notes—
is definitely a perk of the job. Record an interaction here.

ANATOMY OF
ME AT WORK

Our "work selves" are very specific versions of us. Illustrate yours.

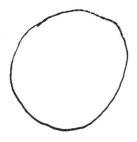

POWER
PONYTAIL

ALWAYS
COLD

3PM —
COFFEE

OUCH

SOUNDTRACK: _____

_____

_____

_____

AFTERNOON SNACK: _____

_____

_____

SECRET WEAPON: _____

_____

_____

DAYDREAM: _____

_____

_____

POWER OUTFIT: _____

_____

_____

INTeRacTioN WiTH
A STRANGeR

Record a fun, interesting, or magical exchange
with someone totally new to you.

A Decision in 3 Acts

Illustrate your mental process from an idea to execution, to the result
of a decision here—maybe you changed your life, or your skin care routine.

1. Think

2. Feel

3. Go

MY MORNING BRAIN

What is on your mind when you wake up?

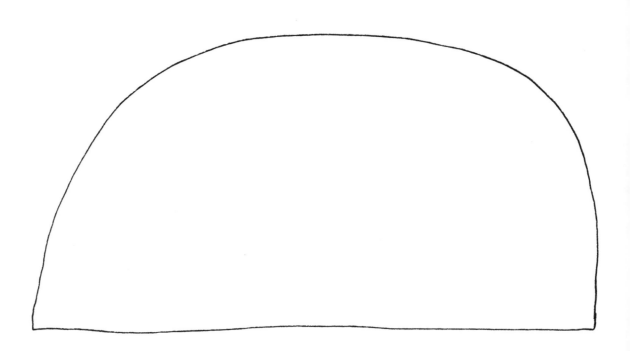

MY ABoUT-To-Fall-ASLeeP
BRAiN

What fills your head at night?

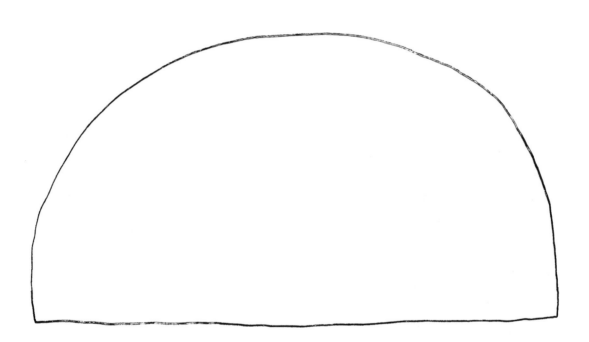

BReaKiNG THRouGH
MY WALL

What's something you've always wanted to do?
Assert yourself against the voice that's holding you back.

MY oBSTACle:

_____

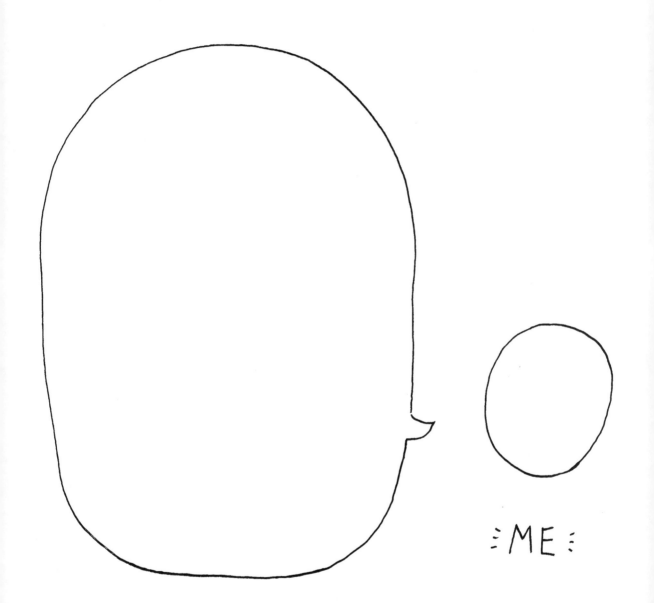

:ME:

MY DAILY ROUTINE

Annotate the clock to show your daily routine.

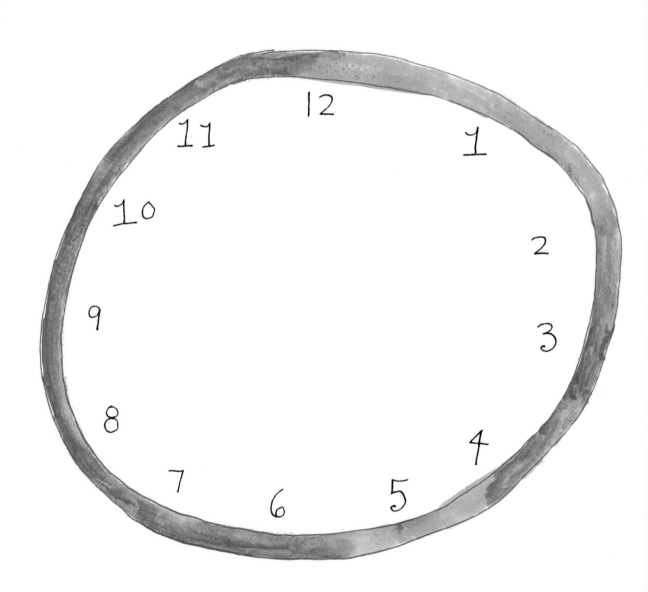

WHAT I WANT MORE OF: _____

_____

_____

_____

_____

_____

_____

_____

WHAT I WANT LESS OF: _____

_____

_____

_____

_____

_____

_____

_____

My FRieNDSHiP wiTH

_____

Map out a close friendship in your life. Think about how it began,
times you got closer, and times when things got tough.

Beginning: How We MeT

_____
_____
_____

WHAT I LoveD ABouT
THeM AT FiRST:

_____
_____
_____

We CoNNecTeD oveR:

_____
_____
_____

WHeRe We ARe NoW:

_____

_____

_____

_____

_____

_____

How We've HELPeD EACH oTHER:

_____

_____

_____

_____

_____

_____

SoMeTHing We DiSAGRee oN:

_____

_____

_____

To-Do List

=HEALTH EDITION=

☐ PHYSICAL: _____

_____

_____

_____

_____

_____

☐ SOCIAL: _____

_____

_____

_____

_____

_____

☐ MENTAL: _____

_____

_____

_____

_____

_____

_____

☐ EMOTIONAL: _____

_____

_____

_____

_____

ANaToMy oF :

Draw a portrait of a friend you admire. Capture their style and their personality!

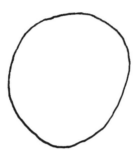

Brilliant

Great Style

Generous

HOBBieS: _____

_____

_____

STReNGTHS: _____

_____

_____

QualiTieS: _____

_____

_____

_____

STYLe: _____

_____

_____

WHat Else? _____

_____

_____

ONE OF THE LOVELIEST GIFTS YOU CAN GIVE YOURSELF IS BEING ALONE. I'VE DISCOVERED WHO I AM BY SPENDING TIME IN SOLITUDE AND LEARNING HOW TO BRAVE TOUGH SITUATIONS AS WELL AS ENJOY INCREDIBLE BEAUTY ALL BY MYSELF. MY FAVORITE WAYS TO BE IN SOLITUDE: SOLO TRAVEL, TAKING MYSELF OUT TO DINNER, AND JOURNALING. LOVING YOUR OWN COMPANY IS A WONDERFUL TOOL YOU CAN USE YOUR WHOLE LIFE, ESPECIALLY DURING CHALLENGING TIMES WHEN YOU NEED SPACE TO REFLECT ON YOUR OWN.

FRee Space

Free Space

FRee Space

FRee Space

My :SoLiTuDe: HeaRT

What goes on in your heart when you're by yourself?

ESCAPE INTO A BooK

ROMANCING MYSELF

CARING FOR MY BODY

TRYING SOMETHING NEW: MY PROGRESS

Think of something you've always wanted to try—cooking, applying a smoky eye, surfing—and chart your progress here. If you like, plot specific triumphs along the way.

PROGRESS

TIME

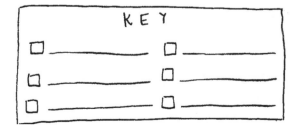

KEY

PROGRESS

TIME

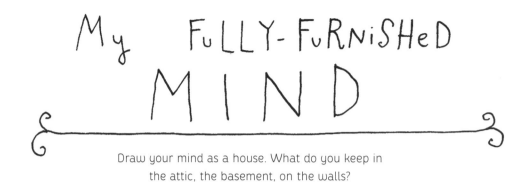

My FuLLY-FuRNiSHeD MIND

Draw your mind as a house. What do you keep in
the attic, the basement, on the walls?

THe ATTic:

CHiLDHooD MeMoRieS:

VACATioN
MEMORiES

PAST LoVeS:

HoLiDAYS:

HiGH SCHooL:

GROUND FLOOR:

DREAMS

GRATITUDE

LOVED ONES

THOUGHTS

BASEMENT:

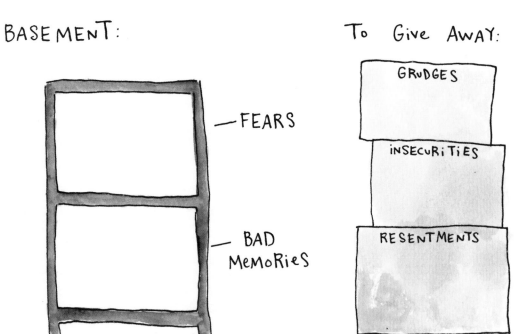

— FEARS

— BAD MEMORIES

To GIVE AWAY:

GRUDGES

INSECURITIES

RESENTMENTS

My Life in Books

Arrange these shelves with books that have been important, challenging, and inspirational for you through the years.

CHILDHOOD:

AGeS
0-5

AGeS
5-10

WHaT MaKeS ME :ME:

How have you defined yourself after the years?

IDeNTiFieR:

YEAR:

IDeNTiFieR:

YEAR:

IDenTiFieR:

YEAR:

IDenTiFieR:

YEAR:

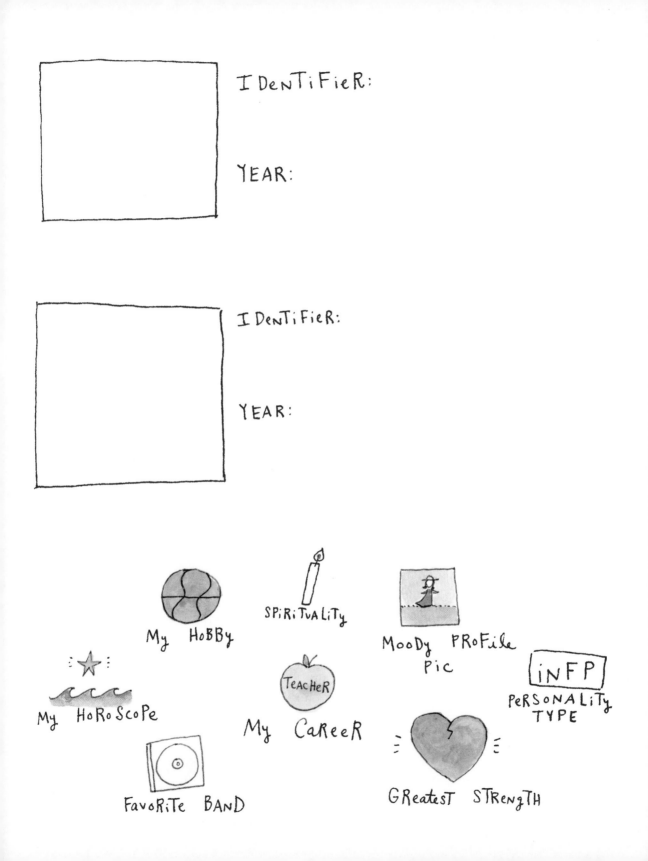

My HoBBy

SPiRiTuALiTy

MooDy PRoFile
Pic

My HoRoScoPe

TEACHER

My CaReeR

iNFP

PeRSoNALiTy
TYPE

FavoRiTe BAND

GReatest STRengTH

The Best Moments on My Journey
Toward Adulthood were not "Important"
MileStones, But Rather The SLOW
Meandering Saturdays Spent Walking
Around The City, Exploring and Observing.
It's Easy To Feel Like you HAVE To
Figure iT ALL ouT, But THen You
overLook The Sweet, Small Moments
That ARE Much MoRe VALuABLe
in HinDSiGHT.

To-Do List

⁝ NEW THINGS ⁝

Do you ever think, "I wish I were the kind of person who. . . ."?
Today's the day to begin being that person!

THING TO TRY	STEP 1
☐	☐
☐	☐
☐	☐
☐	☐

MY FOOD PyRAMiD

What comprises most of your diet and what do you eat sparingly?
Draw it all here.

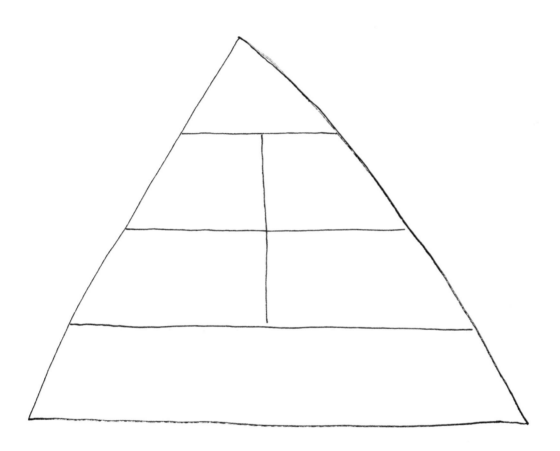

MeRLoT

HoT SAUCE

BAGeLS

TACoS

WASABi PEAS

SPARKLiNG WATeR

A TexT I wiSH I CouLD SEND

Here's your opportunity to write a hate text you know you shouldn't send, but you need to get out of your system.

My ꞊ Happy Place꞊ HeART

Where is your happy place? What feelings does it evoke?

My Life ReStauRant

Create a "restaurant" of your memories. Put your most memorable meals on the menu.

MENU

CHILDHOOD FavoRiTe:

FaMily SPecialTY:

VacaTioN MEMoRY:

My DAiLy BREAKFaST:

GReaT DATE:

Now DRaw youR FAVORiTe MEAL:

THE MUSEUM OF MY LIFE

If someone were to visit the museum of you, what would they see? You are the curator!
Which artifacts, busts, paintings, and diorama would you include?

STILL LIFE FROM MY HOME

THE BUST OF
AN IMPORTANT
FIGURE IN MY LIFE

COLLECTION OF ARTIFACTS
FROM SPECIAL MOMENTS

:ME:
AS A STATUE

PORTRAIT OF SOMEONE
WHO HAS BEEN THERE FOR ME

AN ABSTRACT PAINTING OF MY MOOD

DIORAMA OF A HAPPY MEMORY FROM MY CHILDHOOD

ONE OF THE BEST DATING TIPS I GOT
IN MY TWENTIES WAS "DON'T THINK ABOUT
WHETHER YOU'RE RIGHT FOR THIS PERSON;
THINK ABOUT WHETHER THIS PERSON IS
RIGHT FOR YOU." SO, FEEL FREE TO MAKE
THE JOKE THAT MIGHT NOT LAND, WEAR
THE OUTFIT THAT MAKES YOU FEEL AMAZING,
TELL THE STORIES THAT ARE IMPORTANT
TO YOU. IF THEY ARE THE RIGHT FIT,
YOU'LL BOTH BE GRATEFUL THAT YOU WERE
ABLE TO BRING YOUR WHOLE, SPARKLING,
BEAUTIFUL SELF TO THE TABLE.

MaKiNG AMeNDS WiTH
THe MoNSTeR oF ME

What's something you've said that you know hurt someone else?
What would you say to that "demon" now?

≡ ME THeN ≡

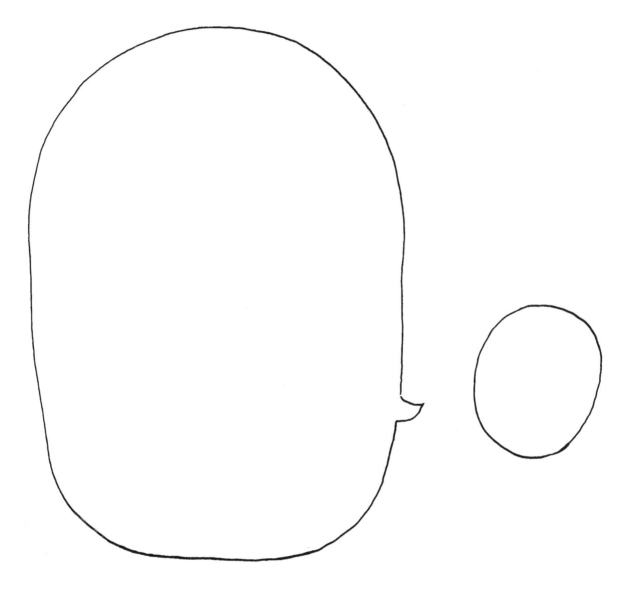

:ME NOW:

My INTeReSTS

Label your hobbies or passions in the key, then graph how your interests have grown or shrunk over time.

INTeReST

TiME

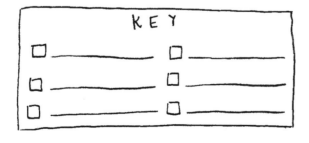

KEY

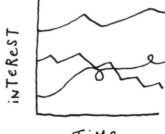

iNTeReST

TiMe

CReATiViTy iN 3 AcTS

{THE iDEA} Time ♪ SHARe ♪

Creativity often begins long before you actually make anything.
What does creativity feel like for you? Document the three-step process below.

1. INSPiRaTioN

2. ExecuTioN

3. CReaTioN

MY ALTeRNate Lives

What did you used to want to be when you "grew up"? What are some other
paths you could have taken? Zoom in on each of those alternate lives.

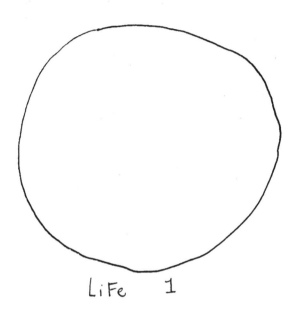

Jo B:

CiTy:

LiFeSTyLe:

LiFe   1

JoB:

CiTy:

LiFeSTyLe:

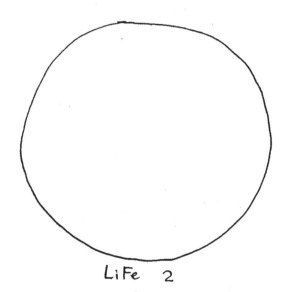

LiFe   2

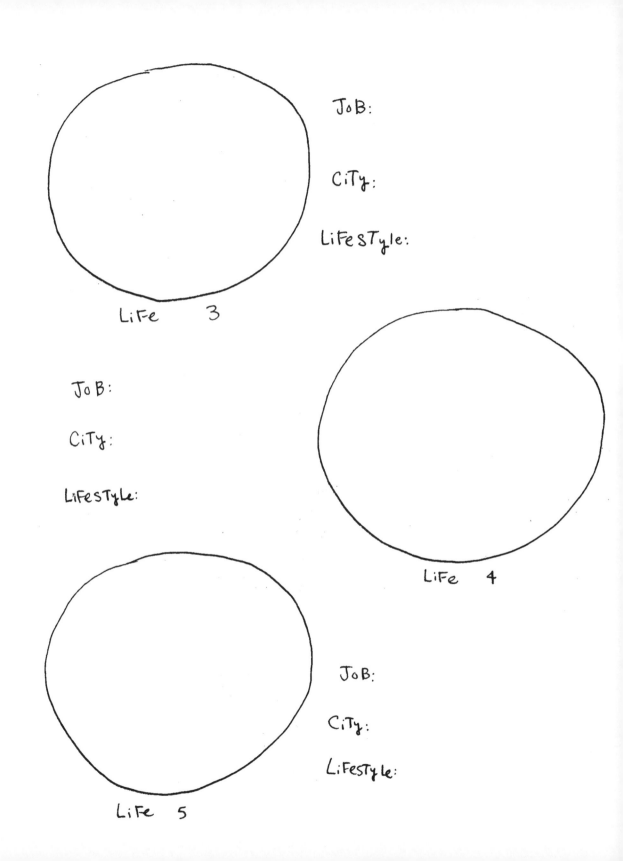

JOB:

CiTy:

LiFeSTyle:

LiFe   3

JoB:

CiTy:

LiFeSTyle:

LiFe   4

JoB:

CiTy:

LiFeSTyle:

LiFe   5

WEaTheR RePoRT

Weather sets the perfect backdrop for specific feelings, music, and activities.
Attach your own feelings to specific types of weather.

SuNSHiNe:

_____

_____

oveRCAST:

_____

_____

WiND:

_____

_____

CRiSP:

_____

_____

R A i N :

_____

_____

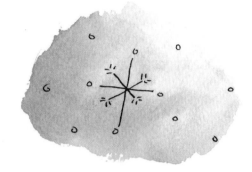

S N O W :

_____

_____

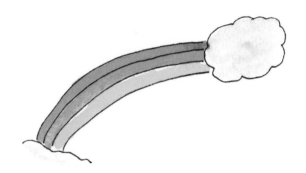

AFTeR The RAiN:

_____

_____

F O G :

_____

_____

CARing FoR YouRSeLF

A big moment that carried two competing emotions
at once (e.g., graduation, a big move).

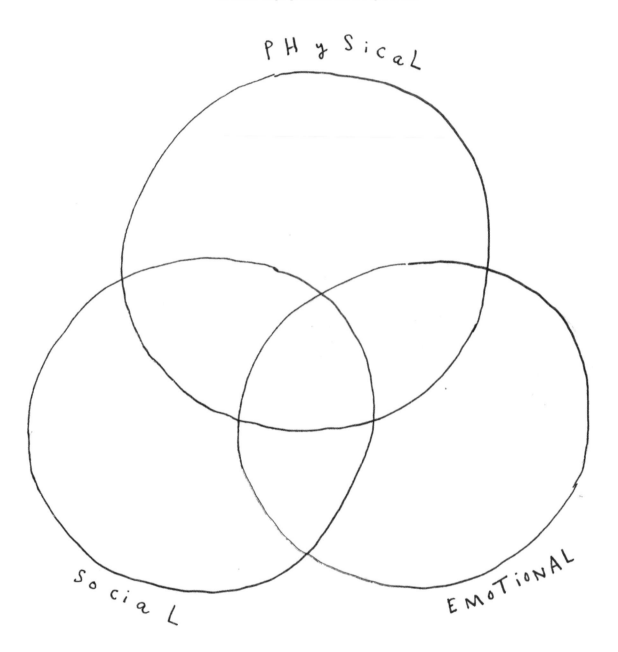

PHySicaL

SociaL

EMoTioNAL

TRanSLaTion, PLeASe!

You probably talk about the same topic very differently with two different friends.

TOPic: _____

WHAT I'D
SAY To:

_____

WHAT I'D
SAY To:

_____

My _____ AS a FiLM SET

Choose a space you frequent—perhaps your block, or desk—
and draw it as a set, complete with props and a wardrobe.

PROPS

FOOD OR DRINK: _____

_____

_____

HOME DÉCOR: _____

_____

_____

ELECTRONICS: _____

_____

WARDROBE: _____

_____

_____

IN MY BAG: _____

_____

_____

To-Do List

≡ BEFORE I TURN ___ ≡

☐ Place I want To Go:

_____

_____

☐ Experience I want To Have:

Ticket _____

_____

☐ Thing I want To Learn:

PORTUGUESE

_____

_____

☐ How I want To Grow:

_____

_____

FRee Space

FRee Space

FRee Space

FRee Space

CONSTRUCTIVE CRITICISM

Call out a piece of criticism that felt particularly harsh,
but true. What good can you find hidden in it?

THe CRITiQue

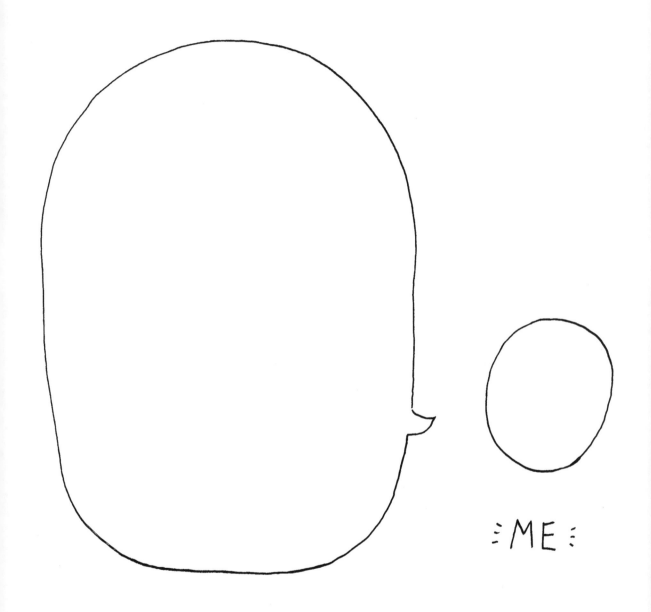

My ꞊HEALeD꞊ HeaRT

Rejection, an illness, or anything else—fill your heart with
everything that helped you through the process.

CREATIVITY IN 3 ACTS

Create a visual metaphor for a goal you have.

1. INSPIRATION

2. EXECUTION

3. CREATION

My FavoRiTe WAY To CALM MySeLF

No matter the stressor, we all have ways to self-soothe.
Illustrate your emotional state before and after entering yourself?

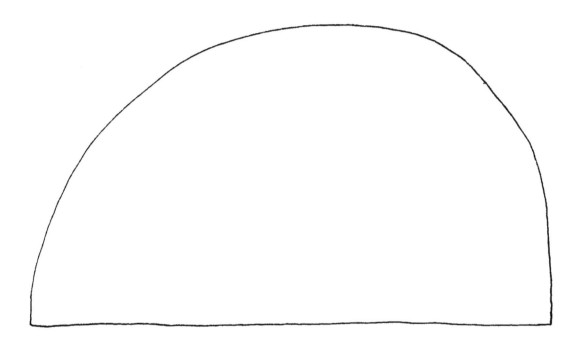

MY   BRAiN   BeFoRe

How   ThiS   ActiviTy   MAKeS   ME   FeeL

WHaT'S STRESSiNG Me ouT:

_____

_____

_____

My BRAiN AFTeR

CREATING MY
PERSonal OASiS

Even if you live with five other people, parts of your home are just yours.
Capture those favorite spaces—real or imagined.

READiNg Nook

FAVoRiTe Place
To SiT

PET oR PLaNT

SPeciAL SHeLF

FAVoRiTe oR IDeAL
WALL CoLoR

WALL   ART

COLLECTION

MEDICINE CABINET

BEAUTY   PRODUCTS

MEMORY   BOX

TRINKET

VANITY

My Life in HeART BReakS

List the things you've learned from different types of heartbreak
(e.g., falling out with a friend, rejections from schools or jobs, missed opportunities).

HeaRTBReak:

SiLveR LiNiNG:

HeaRTBReak:

New DooR THAT oPeneD:

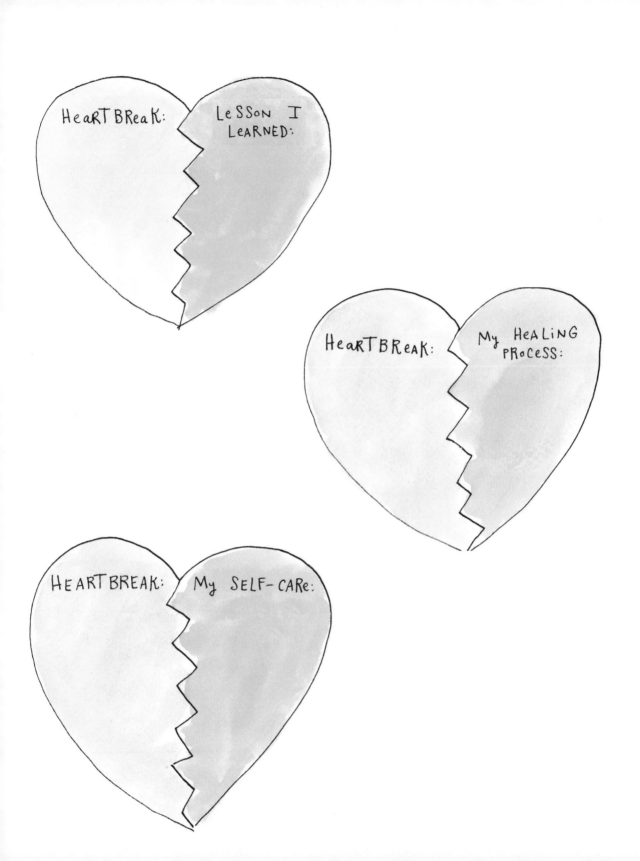

My Mood
THRoUGHouT The DAY

Do you light up with creative energy in the morning, the middle of the day,
or at night? Graph your energy levels and moods throughout the day.
If you like, note what makes it shift.

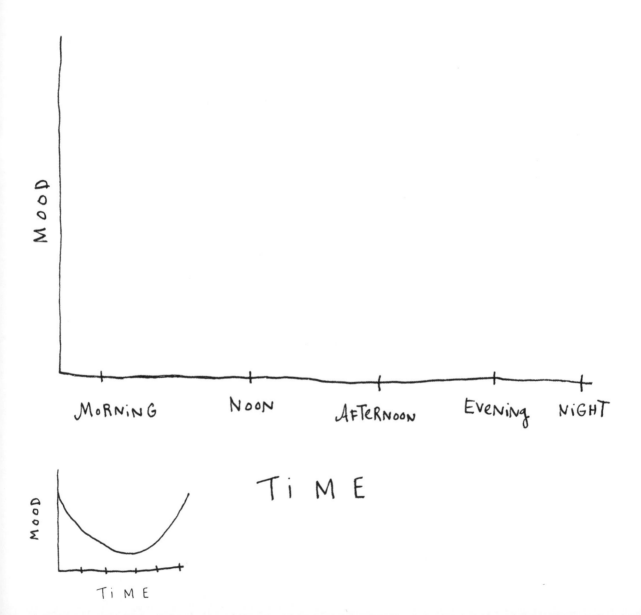

MOOD

MORNING   NOON   AFTERNOON   EVENING   NIGHT

TiME

MooD

TiME

FRee Space

Free Space

FRee Space

Free Space

MY COZY LIST

List the things that make your heart feel warm and fuzzy.

COZIEST OUTFIT:

_____

_____

COZIEST MOVIE:

_____

_____

COZIEST BOOK:

_____

_____

COZIEST ACTIVITY:

_____

_____

CoZiesT FRieND:

CoZiesT WEATHeR:

_____

_____

CoZiesT TiMe
oF DAY:

CoZiesT FooD:

_____

_____

MYSELF

AS DiRecTeD By _____

Draw yourself "as directed by" someone who made your favorite TV show or movie, or authored your favorite book. How do you look as a character in that setting?

As directed
by Wes Anderson

My CHaRacTeR'S...

PRoPS: _____

_____

_____

FRienDS / Love inTeReST: _____

_____

_____

PRoFeSSioN: _____

_____

_____

OPinioN oN My LiFe: _____

_____

_____

_____

A MeMoRy
FROM MY inBox

Record a memorable e-mail exchange.

To:

From:

Subject:

The gist:

_____

_____

_____

_____

_____

How it made me feel:

_____

_____

_____

_____

_____

CReaTiNG MYSeLF
iN ✸ 🔍 👑 3 AcTS

Finding yourself is actually an exercise in creativity.
Use three visuals to illustrate how you arrived at "yourself."

1. EXPeRiMenT

2. DiScoveRy

3. AcTuALizaTioN

My RoManTic HeaRT

Fill your heart with the feelings, memories, gestures,
sensations, and hopes you have when you fall in love.

CANDLe. LiGHT

TexTS

SUNDAY MoRNING

LiPSTick

HeSiTATioN

My PaRenTal FiGuRES

What are the traits you share with your
parents/two parental figures?

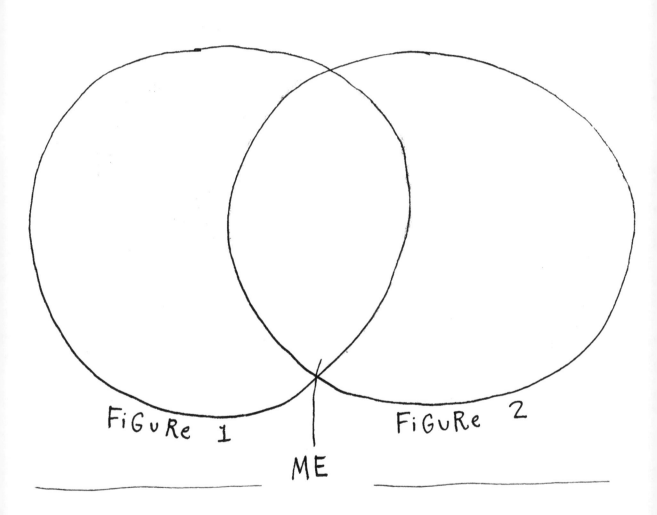

FiGuRe 1   FiGuRe 2

ME

A BAD EXPERIENCE

Do you have a bad memory or unfortunate experience that keeps you from trying something over again? How can you banish it?

MY MEMORY:

_____

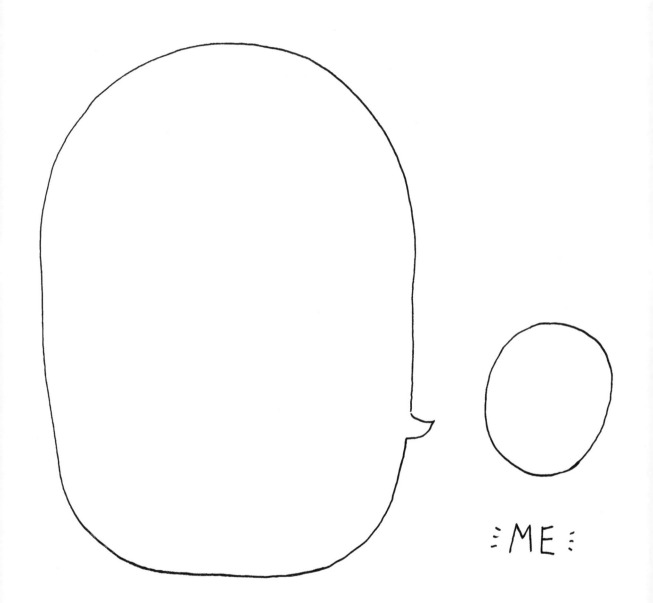

MY HOMETOWN

If you've moved away from home, chances are it looks pretty different when
you visit now than when you lived there. How do the two compare?
Home might be the town you grew up in, a college campus,
or the block your first adult dwelling was on.

WELCOME TO

(_ YEARS AGO)

I've MoveD AROuND A LoT, So I've
Had Many PeRiodS oF LoneLiNeSS—
uN SuRe oF WHat I waS Doing
AND STRuggLinG To MaKe SENSE
oF a New CiTy AND Social ATMoSPHeRe.
I've FouND THat I Had To TAKe
TheSe MoMeNTS Really SLowLy. SoMeTiMES
THat MeanS MAKing FRieNDS WHo WouLDNT
LaST PAST A CouPle MoNTHS, oR TaKing
A JoB I MigHT RealiZe I HaTED
aFTeR Two WeeKS. ITs OKAy. AS
Long aS youRe LEARNiNg FRoM EACH
ExPeRieNCe, NoNe oF iT iS WASTeD TiME.

Places I've Lived

Record all the places you've lived. Maybe it's lots of different towns and cities, or maybe it's super-specific spots that shaped you.

WHeRe My FAMiLy iS:

WHeRe I MeT My BeST FRieND:

WHeRe I BecAMe MySeLF:

WHeRe I LeARNED THe MoST:

WHERE I FELL
IN LOVE:

_____

WHERE I
EXPERIENCED SADNESS:

_____

WHERE I HEALED:

_____

WHERE I HOPE
TO GO NEXT:

_____

MY DReaM BLocK

If all your favorite shops, cafés, and homes were
on a single street, what would it look like?

Thinking of YOU

Here are eight bouquets of flowers for individuals or groups of people on your mind. Who would appreciate these warm thoughts?

_____

_____

_____

_____

_____

_____

_____

_____

MY EMOTIONAL STATE
THROUGHOUT THE YEAR

Which months drag you down while others rejuvenate you?
Chart them here, and plot specific moments if you'd like.

Mood

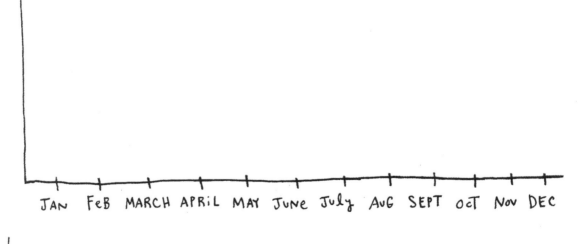

JAN   FEB   MARCH   APRIL   MAY   JUNE   July   AUG   SEPT   OCT   NOV   DEC

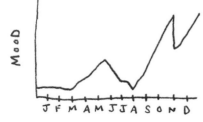

To - Do List
≡ FOR THIS SEASON ≡

☐ To WeAR: _____

_____

☐ To Do: _____

_____

☐ To See: _____

_____

NOW SHOWING

☐ To Listen To: _____

_____

☐ To EAT: _____

_____

MaGical ThiNGS I've SeeN

iN : _____ :

Record your observations from favorite places.

WARM iNteRACTioN
BeTweeN STRANGeRS:

_____

STyLiSH PeRSoN:

_____

STReeT MusiciAN
MoMenT:

_____

_____

AcT oF KiNDNeSS:

_____

_____

PUBLIC TRANSPORTATION
    OBSERVATION:

_____

_____

CUTE COUPLE   OR
    GOOD FRIENDS:

_____

_____

SOMETHING   BEAUTIFUL:

_____

_____

SOMETHING   HOPEFUL:

_____

_____

My BeST DeciSion

What's a decision you made that changed your life for the better?
Draw your perspective before and after.

My PeRSPecTive on LiFe
BEFoRe I _____

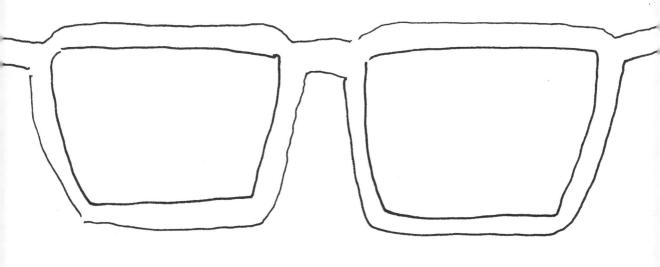

My PeRSPeCTiVe oN LiFe
AFTeR

A STORM IN 3 ACTS

What's a situation in your life that could be described
using the phases of a storm?

1. The CALM

2. THe STORM

3. The AFTERMATH

IT'S alwayS HELPeD Me To WRiTe
DowN all THe THiNgS aNd PeoPle
THat iNSPiRe ME, aNd I uSe THiS
LiST To CReate My iLLuSTRaTioNS
aND ESSAYS. I ReviSiT iT oFTeN.
TheRe iS No RiGHT Way To BE
iNSPiReD; FiND iT iN AnyTHiNG THat
GiveS youR HeaRT A LiTTle LiFT oR
MakeS you WANT To TAKe a SeCoND
Look.

THE BEST COMEBACK
I NEVER SAID

Think of an argument you had where you thought of an amazing comeback AFTER the conversation was over. Record it here!

MY GREMLIN:

_____

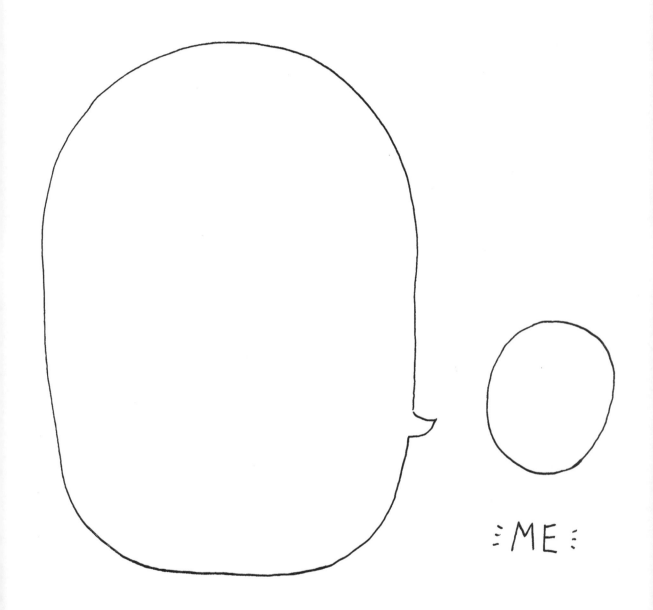

MY RELATIONSHIP
CURRENCY

List the ways that you "exchange" love and care between
you and your friends, like when you bring them coffee or
when they show up at your improv show.

CURRENCY: _____
PERSON: _____

_____

CURRENCY: _____
PERSON: _____

_____

CURRENCY: _____
PERSON: _____

_____

CURRENCY: _____
PERSON: _____

_____

CURRENCY: _____
PERSON: _____
_____

CURRENCY: _____
PERSON: _____
_____

CURRENCY: _____
PERSON: _____
_____

CURRENCY: _____
PERSON: _____
_____

ANaToMy oF The MAiN
CHARacTeR iN My NoVEL

If you've ever dreamed of writing fiction, start here.
What does your main character look like?

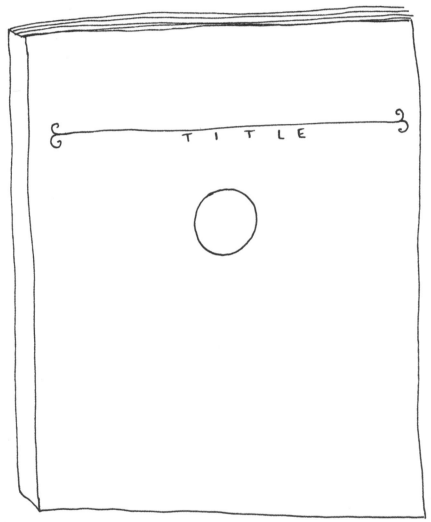

T I T L E

CHARACTER PROFILE:

NAME: _____

BOOK TITLE: _____

HOME: _____

_____

JOB: _____

_____

CHALLENGES: _____

_____

DESIRES: _____

_____

STYLE: _____

_____

My CiRcuLAR THouGHT PRoceSS

What's the same conclusion you always make?
Illustrate a recurring spiraling thought.

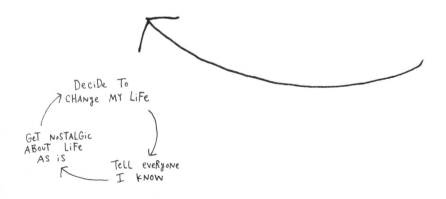

DeciDe To CHANge MY LiFe

GeT NoSTALGic ABouT LiFe AS iS

TeLL eveRyoNe I kNOW

MY :Home: HeART

What is home for you?

:MY:
COFFEE
SHOP

SCENTS OF
CINNAMON + SAGE

WALKS THROUGH
THE WOODS

MY LiFe iN FRiEND SHiPS

Record the besties (animals count!) who have gotten you to where you are today.

WHEN WE MET:

WHERE WE MET:

WHAT I LEARNED FROM THEM:

FRiEND:

WHEN WE MET:

WHERE WE MET:

WHAT I LEARNED FROM THEM:

FRiEND:

WHEN WE MET:

WHERE WE MET:

HOW WE'VE GROWN TOGETHER:

FRIEND:

WHEN WE MET:

WHERE WE MET:

CHALLENGE WE FACED TOGETHER:

FRIEND:

WHEN WE MET:

WHERE WE MET:

FAVORITE THING WE HAVE IN COMMON:

FRIEND:

To-Do List

Make The World a Better Place

- [ ] Something I Can Do For a Friend:

  _____

- [ ] Something I can Do For a Stranger:

  _____

- [ ] Something I Can Give:

  _____

- [ ] Something I Can Do For The Earth:

  _____

- [ ] Someone I Can Forgive:

  _____

Free Space

Free Space

Free Space

Free Space

My Emotional Gym

Going through challenges builds up our emotional "muscles" in order to be more resilient in the future. What are some things you've been through that have contributed to the strong heart you have now?

A   Rejection:

_____

_____

A   Disappointment:

_____

_____

A   Bad   Haircut/
Outfit/Makeup   Look:

_____

_____

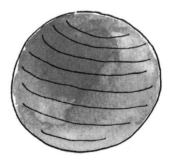

Embarrassment:

_____

_____

LOSS:

_____

_____

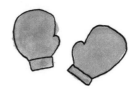

BAD JOB:

_____

_____

TOUGH TRANSITION:

_____

_____

LONELINESS:

_____

_____

My ☰ HoPeFuL ☰ HeART

What are the hopes you have for yourself? What gives you hope?
Reference this page when you're feeling down.

MY HieRARCHY OF NEEDS

What do you need to feel like a productive, creative, and loved person?
It might be friends, or it mught be salty french fries.

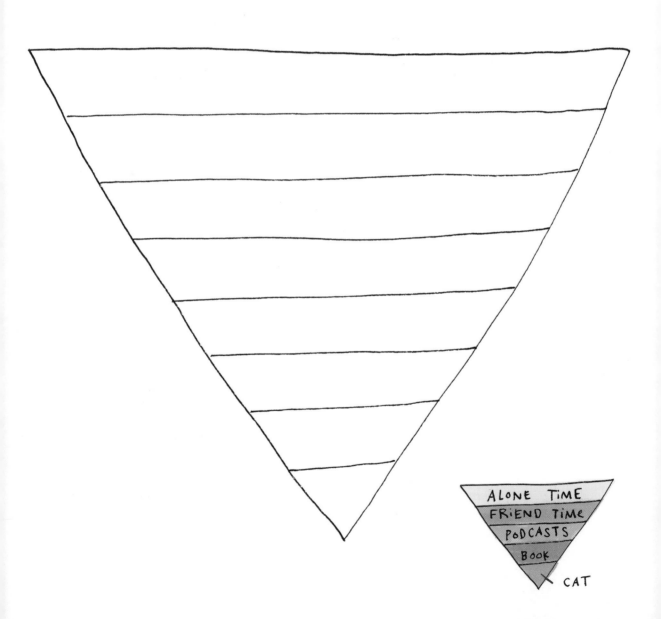

ALONE TIME
FRIEND TIME
PODCASTS
BOOK
CAT

My VOYAGE TOWARD HEALING

Experiencing a heartbreak, illness, or any other kind of pain can feel isolating. On the boats below, write a list of the things that will help connect you to other people and heal.

WHERE I AM NOW

IT's EASY TO SAY "LooK oN THE BRiGHT SiDe," BuT iTs iNCReDiBly DiFFicuLT To Do. ReMaiNiNg OPTiMiSTic aNd PoSiTive iS HaRD WoRK, So you Really HAve To PRACTice at iT. BecoMing A RESiLiENT PeRSoN iSNT aS EASY aS PoweRiNg THRouGH oR "CHooSing HAPPiNeSS," BuT Doing LiTTle THiNgS EveRy Day To KeeP YouR HoPe AFloAT Will HELP you CuLTi VATE GRatiTuDe aNd JOY DuRing ChaLLeNGeS.